For It To Be, It's Up To Me

Visit www.booksurge.com to order additional copies.

For It To Be, It's Up To Me

Simple Ways Of Living A Healthy, Prosperous, Satisfied Life

Sanjeev Aneja

2007

"To be happy." That is the answer most frequently given by people when they are asked their primary desire in life. Yet while many seek happiness, it frequently turns out to be elusive. Most of us are even hard-pressed to define exactly what happiness is.

Not so Sanjeev Aneja, who has been asked many times in his life, "Why are you so satisfied and always positive?" and who now provides the answers in his appealing work, *For It To Be, It's Up To Me.* This upbeat book offers not just one way to make happiness attainable, but 21 gems of sage advice for those of us seeking more satisfaction in life. These helpful words of wisdom are presented in the form of lessons covering a wide range of topics from attitude to gratitude and health to wealth, all of them carefully explored in a way that can make a profound and positive difference.

Aneja's discussion of each lesson touches on many subjects that hold profound meaning for all of us, and yet his fundamental message is that anything is possible to those of us who believe that it is so and then act to make it real. At the same time, we must learn how to be happy with what we have; otherwise, we will never be satisfied because we will always be looking for more in the future.

Aneja walks his talk as a hard-working immigrant from India who studied electrical engineering and is now successfully runs a real estate office. In addition, he is quite active in his community. The lessons he has learned translate well into tools that could be of great value to any reader who wishes to learn the fundamental ways to gain the contentment we all seek.

CONTENTS

AUTHOR'S WISH FOR YOU

Dream big and may all your dreams come true. May God bless you with all that you wish (and what is right for you).

Sanjeev

Sanjeev Aneja
Your well wisher

You can contact me at anytime via my email:
sanjeev@sanjeevaneja.com

Dedicated
to
Lord Krishna

No matter what name we call Him/Her by, He/She exists and that is what matters. It's not about the road we take, it's about the destination we want to get to.

INTRODUCTION

Are you seeking wealth, happiness and peace? Do you want to be physically and mentally healthy so that you can follow your dreams and make them come true? Do you want to be worry free and stress free? Do you have goals that lead you to your dreams, or do you just let each day run your life? If you said yes to any of these questions or if you know of someone who might benefit from the answers to these questions, then this book is for you.

Thank you for making this invaluable book a part of your library and a part of your life. It will transform you if you put it to use on a daily basis. I've tried my best to make this book as simple and direct as possible with a minimum of stories and fancy words that make you consult your dictionary. And here is my promise: If you live these lessons daily, your life will change dramatically, for **good**. As basic as these lessons and advice may seem, it's not going to be easy to accept them or follow them everyday. You will fall into your old patterns often, especially when the challenges are hard and the moments are tough. And it's OK, as long as you can quickly recover from your situation by remembering the lessons learnt and then applying them. If you can do this, you will have benefited from this book.

Our goal should be to become just a little better the next time. And a commitment to become better will undoubtedly lead us to our desired result. My friend T Harv Eker says, "How you do anything is how you do everything". So true. When you commit to do something a little better, you will start doing a lot of things a little better. And it all adds up fast.

Suggestions are easy to give, yet hard to live by. My mentor Jim Rohn, a well-respected philosopher and motivational speaker, says, "Follow what I say but don't follow what I do." I smile and agree with him one hundred percent. At times we will all do differently than we preach. Don't follow those moments. And don't be too hard on yourself when you have such moments. Just learn to recover quickly.

We are not saints who live in an isolated world. Our surroundings and the ongoing demands and needs bring with them the stress of daily living. We become victims of outside forces at times, sometimes without even noticing them. My goal and desire is to bring to you the suggestions that will slowly and gradually transform your life by helping you reduce the effect of the outside world through controlling your inside world. While the causes can't be controlled by us, the effects in almost all cases can be. It takes will, determination, and commitment to do so. And yes, we all have the power to control our actions and thereby achieve the desired results. Remember that although we can't control the actions of others, we can always control our own actions.

To get the most out of this book, I suggest that you read a chapter a day, then complete the action items and affirmations in that chapter. This is not a novel that should be finished in one reading; trying to do so will bring only minimal results. Finishing it quickly in one sitting will not help you accomplish much. Keep a highlighter and a pen with you. Mark your book as much as you can. Write your notes in it. When you are reading, ideas will come to your mind. Jot them down. Then refer to your ideas often.

Let me make a **BOLD** promise here. If you complete this book entirely, one lesson a day including your actions items and affirmations and then apply the suggestions/lessons as if your life depended on them, your personal success story will be by your own design, not by accident. And if I am wrong, simply return the marked book to me, along with the original receipt and your comments on why the book didn't help you, and I will refund your purchase price, no questions asked.

By the way, not all lessons are necessary for everyone. You may already be very good at some of the suggested actions. Therefore they may just be a reinforcement for you, and a quick read will do. Others, you may have to read a few times and implement them to make them a habit. Work at your own pace to make them a part of your life. Commit to being the very best you can be. Don't accept less when more is possible of you.

There is also a possibility that you may not like some of the suggestions given in the book. Please don't tune yourself out at that point. Take everything that helps you and leave the rest behind for me.

Sanjeev Aneja

Start With Gratitude

LESSON I.

Start With Gratitude

"A man was complaining about having no shoes till he saw someone with no feet."

Wake up everyday with a sense of gratitude. Thank God for all you have been blessed with, and thank God for possibilities that lie ahead of you.

In today's hectic world, it is easy to lose sight of all we have. We are always trying to catch up with our neighbors and other friends while forgetting our blessings. And that results in unhappiness. The funny part is, your neighbors and friends are most likely trying to catch up with you, and they are unhappy because of that as well. Happiness lies within us. Happiness lies in recognizing what we have and what we truly need, not in what we want. Our 'wants' keep us from enjoying the present moment. And there is no end to our 'wants.' By the way, there is nothing wrong with 'wants.' Be all you can be, get all you can get, and do all you can do—that is absolutely fine. Just don't lose your happiness, your family, and most importantly, your health, in chasing for what matters least. Be thankful for all you have.

When we are in the 'Thanks' mode, we appreciate every small thing. When in materialistic 'want' mode, we appreciate almost nothing because as soon as we get it, we want more of it, or we want something different/better.

All important things in life are given to us for FREE by God. We must recognize them and be truly thankful for them as well. When we are born, we are blessed (in most cases) with a complete body—two legs, two arms, a heart, two kidneys, two eyes, a nose, two ears—all of them functioning like magic. We are blessed with a billion dollar mind; we are blessed with hope, with power to think and act, and a lot more. What did we do to deserve all that? In the Hindu religion, just like in many other religions, it is said that deeds from our past lives create our current lives. Being born as a human being, in a certain family, in a certain country—these are no coincidences in this universe. We all come into this world and into the lives of others as part of our destiny and karma. We should cherish these moments and be thankful for them, as human life is one of the most blessed of lives, compared to all other living entities. If you believe in reincarnation, if you believe in life after death, then you must also understand that there was a past life for us and that there will be a future life too. Will we come back again as better human beings or will we be an animal, insect or microorganism? We don't know what we will come back as, it all depends upon our deeds in this life and also on the deeds of our past lives. And while we can not control our past lives, we sure can be great human beings in this life. One thing we know for sure is that there is too much to be thankful for in this current life, regardless of our circumstances.

What else can we thank God for on a daily basis? How about the air we breathe (imagine living without oxygen)? The water we drink? The sunlight? The rain? The day? The night?

You get the picture, don't you? And everything we have discussed so far comes for FREE. It's provided to us for FREE by nature, by God.

Spend at least five minutes in the morning while waking up, and five minutes at night when getting ready to sleep, thanking God for his blessings. Be thankful even if you feel you are not blessed with all the things most of us take for granted. Let's say you were born blind or lost your sight when you were very young. Why should you be thankful? Let that not be your attitude. Be thankful for your legs, your arms, your mind. When you see the whole picture and when you analyze what additional senses were granted to you by God due to the lack of eyesight, you will be amazed. Be thankful for what you have, always. You will discover a new you when you do that.

Having an attitude of gratitude grants us peace. Notice your breath and observe the peace when you are thankful for what you have. And notice your feelings and your mood at that point too. Doesn't it feel wonderful?

What if you are stuck in traffic and late to work? Should you be thankful then? And why should you be thankful in such a situation? How about imagining that there is a serious accident ahead of you with few passengers critically injured and that the traffic is blocked because they are trying to get those people to the closest hospital? Can you be thankful for not being part of that accident? Can you be thankful for not being the reason for that accident? How do you feel when you put things in that perspective? The traffic jam won't frustrate you much at all anymore. In fact the feeling of gratitude will change you from being upset to being thankful and peaceful. The focus will change from "Why Me?" to "Thank God, It's Not Me".

One other thing you can do to be peaceful and happy in this otherwise materialistic and stressful world is to remember God at all times, especially when things are going well. Think of Him, say His name, repeat His name often (that's called Japa or Mantra). You can do Japa when you are in the shower, when you are driving, when you are stuck in traffic, and at all other possible moments.

My favorite Japa comes from Hindu religion. It is:
Hare Ram Hare Ram (her a raam)
Ram Ram Hare Hare
Hare Krishna Hare Krishna (her a krish na)
Krishna Krishna Hare Hare

For those who follow Christianity in the orthodox tradition, the Japa could be
Lord Jesus Christ, Son of God, have mercy on me

In Judaism, the Japa could be
Barukh Atah Adonai

In Buddhism, it could be
Om mami padme hum

In Islam, it could be
Allahu Akbar

All you have to do is remember God and repeat His name.

Talk to your religious leader and ask for the appropriate Japa. Follow the words that come from your religious belief. Then repeat them over and over, and you will soon discover peace. And by the way, please don't be caught up in "my God Vs his God". God is one, regardless of what name we call Him by.

I am often asked, "If we are always satisfied and happy due to our gratitude and appreciation of what we have, how will we ever progress, as we will have nothing to look forward to?" It's a great question and a logical one. But nowhere did I say that you don't aim high. Nowhere did I suggest that you not gather material things. Nowhere did I say that you should not compete to be the best. In fact, this whole book is about you shaping your destiny and living a life you deserve, a lifestyle you choose to live.

Gratitude is about being thankful for what we have and enjoying all we have. Many of us get so caught up in our day-to-day living, or in the pursuit of more and more, that we forget to enjoy today's blessings. Being thankful helps us recognize and enjoy what we have now instead of being unhappy about what we don't have yet, or what we may lose tomorrow.

If only many rich and famous people had followed this advice before they committed suicide. If only they had counted their blessings and thanked God for being blessed with all the basic necessities of life (things that they had no control over yet were fortunate to have), and then a lot more. Money may give us luxuries, but it can never give us happiness. What good is the most expensive bed but restless nights? What good is the availability of the most expensive food yet the doctor's advice not to eat it due to bad health? What good is having a huge home but no one to go home to? Money is very important for most things, but it is useless for things it can't buy. It can't buy love, it can't buy peace of mind, it can't buy happiness. These things can only be achieved through gratitude.

Be thankful to God everyday for all your blessings! Don't complain about things you don't have or ask for things you want; simply recognize what you have and say a few words of appreciation everyday. May God bless you with the power to be thankful for all you have and thereby grant you peace and serenity. One small advice—please do not follow a religion or a preacher blindly. Be very careful in choosing whom you follow, if you follow anyone at all except God.

"An attitude of gratitude makes a huge impact on your happiness."
Be thankful in all circumstances.

<u>Daily Affirmations:</u>
(Please replace God or Krishna or Rama with words appropriate to your spiritual beliefs and religious associations)

God, I am thankful to you for all I have.

Krishna, all that I have is yours and is there to serve you.

God, I thank you for this life, and I promise to make it worthwhile for the good of others.

Rama, thank you for fresh air, food, water, working body parts, a working mind, and so much more.

<u>Action Plan:</u>

1.   Thank God for all the things you are blessed with. Do this when you wake up and before you start your day. Also do this when you lie in bed and are ready to go to sleep.

2.   Say your Japa everyday, as often as you can. In the shower, while struck in traffic, whenever the opportunity exists.

3.   Write a list of all the things that you might have taken for granted but now know how important they are. Include the physical, material, spiritual, nature, family, and other important aspects of your life. Add to this list daily and make this list part of item 1.

Start With Gratitude

Take Care of Your Health

LESSON 2.

Take Care of Your Health

"People carefully select food for their pets and gas for their cars, yet they pay no attention to what goes in their body."

Our physical well-being has an effect on almost all areas of our lives. Have you ever noticed your attitude when you are feeling unhealthy? You are irritable, you make more mistakes, you simply have no interest in anything, and you are willing to spend every penny you have to get your health back.

So why then are we so negligent with our health when it is good? Perhaps we feel that we are not vulnerable to the side effects and after effects of our negligence. Truth is, we pay for our mistakes. Sooner or later, negligence catches up with all of us.

While we can't avoid all health-related problems, many can be controlled and/or prevented. Here are a few simple and easy things to put into our daily practice that can help us stay healthy.

- A daily walk/jog
- A balanced healthy diet
- Vegetarian food
- Small meals
- No smoking
- An apple a day

- A multivitamin a day
- Proper breathing
- Meditation
- Stress reduction exercises
- A positive attitude
- Smiles and laughs

I love Jim Rohn's quote, "What's easy to do is easy not to." So true, isn't it? It's easy to eat an apple a day. It's also easy not to. It's easy to walk a mile a day; it's also easy not to. The choice is always ours.

"For it to be, it's up to me," until you adopt this attitude, outside influences will make it difficult to do what otherwise is so simple. All it takes is a commitment from your end to take control of your life for your sake. Then it takes some effort and action on your part to follow through on your commitment

Walking daily has been proven to be the best exercise again and again. And it's easy for most of us. Yet it's amazing how many of us will drive around the parking lot, for as long as it takes, to find the closest parking spot to the mall entrance. All this to avoid what is good for us—a walk. Park your car as far away as you can, and then walk to the mall. If you park close to the mall because of safety issues, that's different. But don't look for the closest spot just because of the convenience of less walking. Make walking a habit, wherever and whenever possible.

Walk daily. If, for whatever reason, you can't walk daily, do it few times a week on a routine. Do it in the morning or afternoon or evening, based on your work schedule. Walk in the park or on a treadmill. Take the steps instead of an elevator. Every bit helps. Of course, if you have any health related problems, you must consult your doctor to ensure walking will be OK.

Proper breathing is a huge contributor to good health, yet most of us breathe incorrectly. Ample intake of oxygen is very important for our body cells, for energy, and for our well being.

Here is the correct way to breathe. Take a deep breath in and count up to four while doing so. Your tummy should inflate when you breathe in. Now hold your breath in for the count of four (longer if you can, say up to six or eight). And finally, release the breath slowly while your tummy deflates (counts of six to eight will be great). Repeat this eight to ten times in a row and repeat this three to four times daily. Try to incorporate this into your daily schedule three to four times daily, preferably before meals or an hour or two afterwards. If you feel uncomfortable in the beginning, reduce the breathing durations and do it for lesser times. Also, if any health problems prevent you from performing these breathing exercises, consult your doctor.

Overweight is another critical issue. The problem in America is not malnutrition, it is obesity; it is not lack of food, it is too much junk food. Large fries, super large soft drinks, and bigger portions of cakes and ice creams, as tempting as they may be, they are our worst enemies. Watch your diet, and eat smaller meals even if someone else is paying for them or even if it's an all-you-can-eat buffet. Avoid super sizing your meals just because they are only ten cents more than the normal sized meal. When eating, chew a lot. Chewing helps you slow down and prevents you from eating too much. Also, it is good for your digestive system.

But how about an occasional high calorie meal? Sure, why not! Occasional indulgence is fine as long as it doesn't become a habit. But that should be an exception, not a rule. And if you consume a high calorie meal one day, make sure you burn it off quickly with exercise on the same day or the next. Keep your weight under control. Too many extra pounds result in many problems, including cardiac arrests.

Eat less during nighttime. If you overeat at one meal, skip the next one or two, or at least eat less. Fasting is a good way to give your body a break. If fasting is not possible due to illness or disease, eat lightly, limiting yourself to fruits and vegetables. One other recommendation for your digestive system, drink water (or any other liquid) before the meal, rarely during the meal, and never after it, for at least an hour. This advice came from my grandfather, who said that drinking before the meal works like holy water; during, as fatty oil; and immediately after, like poison. Take my Grandpa's advise (ayurveda suggests the same too).

Remember, we are what we eat and we are what we think. Be a careful eater and be a positive thinker under all circumstances. What you think, just like what you eat, has a major effect on your health. We'll discuss this in detail in some of the lessons.

"An Apple a day keeps the doctor away."
And if that's true, why not have an apple everyday?

Daily Affirmations:

My health is very important to me.

I watch my diet everyday.

I only eat healthy foods.

I do not smoke.

I walk and exercise daily.

P.S. Please follow your physician's advice on what corrective measures are right for you. Revise your affirmations accordingly.

Action Items:

I.   My evaluation of my health today indicates:
     (Write down all things you are not satisfied with—
     overweight, lack of stamina, high cholesterol, etc. Be
     very specific: how much overweight, etc.)

2. I can correct the above problems by doing:
(Again, be specific. Your actions could be reducing the intake of food, stopping smoking, etc.)

3. The reasons I haven't taken these corrective actions so far are:

4. Effective today, I will take the following actions to be in shape:

Start With Gratitude

Your Attitude Determines Your Destiny

Take Care of Your Health

LESSON 3.

Your Attitude Determines Your Destiny

"It is not our circumstances but how we respond to them that determines our outcome."

At any given moment, we have a choice. In fact, we have many choices. And the choices we make lead us to the results we get—desirable results, neutral results, or undesirable results.

Choices made with a positive frame of mind will almost always result in desirable results, while those made when negativity and anger are the dominating factors will almost always produce undesirable results.

There are many books written on the topic of a positive attitude. And there are many real life situations of those who, through their positive attitude, changed outcomes that were otherwise impossible to achieve. When life delivered lemons, these real life heroes turned them into lemonade, while many who were in similar situations to theirs messed up their life completely, blaming it all on their circumstances. And then there are those who have everything going for them but who, through their negative attitudes, mess it all up! Which category are you in? If your attitude is always positive, you are way ahead of the game. If you tend to be more negative, then it's not very difficult to make a commitment to slowly change your outlook and act accordingly to achieve better results.

In today's negative world, it is hard to avoid negativity unless you make an effort to do so. I suggest that you stop watching the news, and stop reading the newspapers. They hardly report positive things because positive doesn't sell. The headline that reads "11-year-old kidnapped by 19-year-old" far outsells the headline that reads "19-year-old helps 11-year-old achieve A+ grades." Our environment, our surroundings, and what we listen to and associate with all effect our thinking immensely. Put yourself in an environment of crooks, and you will start acting like one. Be in the middle of saints, and your thoughts become as pure as theirs. No wonder so many newcomer politicians enter office with good intentions of changing the environment yet succumb to the environment themselves.

At any given moment, we have a choice to see the glass half full or half empty. A half empty viewpoint results in dissatisfaction and anger, while a half full interpretation results in thankfulness and happiness. Same amount in the glass, two different outcomes. Why? Because there are two different perspectives, two different thoughts. One is of plenty, another, of lack.

Negative thoughts are like weeds. They grow without effort. Just as you don't have to plant seeds to grow weeds, you don't have to try to get negative thoughts. They just naturally come. Unfortunately, this is not the case with positive thoughts. Positive thoughts need to be grown and cultivated. Not only do we need to make sure that we are always in a positive mode, we also need to make deliberate effort to keep on weeding out the negative thoughts as they can easily affect our positive attitude.

As we sow, so shall we reap! Keep sowing positive thoughts so that you reap only positive results.

The external happenings in our life and in this world are the way they are. We have very little control, if any, over such circumstances. But we surely have control over our inner world and its outcome, based on our thoughts and attitude. Our happiness and our actions are in our hands; they are controlled by how we think. The choice is always, always ours. The following story illustrates it well:

A reporter interviewed two grown sons of a man who was always drunk. One son was always drunk while the other never drank at all. The reporter asked the drunk son, "Why do you drink so much?" Instantly, the son replied, "With a dad like this, what else do you expect?" The reporter expected that answer and nodded reaffirming the son's thoughts. But he was curious to ask the same question of the son who never drank. "Why do you not drink at all?" he asked the other son. And he was surprised to hear the exact same answer: "With a dad like this, what else do you expect?' Same circumstances, but two totally different ways of looking at them and thereby absolutely different results. One blamed his problem on dad; the other learnt a lesson from dad's bad experience. Same dad, different attitudes towards the circumstances, thereby different results.

It is not our circumstances that determine our success or failure. It is our attitude towards those circumstances that determines our destiny. There are many people who are born into a poor family and stay poor all their life. On the other hand, there are many others who are born in similar or worse circumstances but change their destiny through the right attitude and actions.

Don't be a victim of your circumstances. Change your circumstances and help others do the same. Don't let anyone tell you that you can't be a success. And don't ruin anyone's life by telling them that they can't. Most importantly, never tell yourself that you are a looser, that you can't do it. Always have a "Yes I Can" attitude.

When you are faced with a challenge (we don't call it a problem, we call it a challenge), be thankful to God for it, ask for His guidance and courage, and then look for solutions to that challenge. Know that whatever the outcome, you will only become stronger for future actions. Refuse to become a victim. Remember that everyone out there has a different set of challenges and that many have already gone through what you are going through today. Also know that the only time we have no challenges in life is when we are dead. And if that is the case, which is better: challenges or death? Feels better when put in right perspective, doesn't it? Some have health challenges, some money, some relationship, some a combination, but it is OK. Your attitude towards these challenges must stay positive. The results will follow that attitude.

So is it wrong to have negative thoughts and feelings sometimes? No, not at all. It is normal to react negatively when things are going wrong. The key is to recognize this behavior quickly and then bounce right out of it. Refuse to stay in the negative state a minute longer than you have to. Start thinking of positives that can and will come out of the situation, and then watch those positives come through.

Our internal dialogue with ourselves is the key to our success or failure, happiness or dissatisfaction, peacefulness or restlessness. And this internal dialogue is usually based on our past experiences and experience of others. It is also based on our awareness that we control our internal dialogues, an awareness that comes from the people we associate with and the books we read. And it is based on our spiritual belief system. Knowing that there is life after death (reincarnation) helps us act differently compared to a belief system that says that this is it, that there are no future consequences to our current actions. Knowing that who we are in this life is a cumulative sum of our actions in our past lives—and that our actions in this life will affect our future lives—can make a big difference too.

Ponder often on how you talk to yourself. What are you saying to yourself? What answers are you getting back? Are they negative or positive? Be aware and always look for the positive in every situation, no matter how bad it seems at that very moment. The smartest person you can talk to is you. The smartest person you can listen from is you.

Words have enormous power. How would you feel if I said to you, "You are beautiful and you are intelligent and caring too"? Good, right? What if I said, "You are an idiot"? How does that feel? Speaker was the same and so was the listener. Only thing that changed in both the statements was the spoken word. Be careful with the words that you say to yourself. Be careful with the words and messages that you take in from the external sources. Be very, very selective. Refuse to feed garbage into your brain.

Remember that each situation produces different results for different people based on their attitudes and actions towards that situation. Choose to be the one who will only expect positive outcomes through your positive attitude towards life, towards given circumstances, and towards people.

"You have to think any how. Why not make it positive?"
When you expect positive, you will be amazed at how much of it will come your way.

<u>Daily Affirmations:</u>

I am aware of my attitude at all times.

I know that having a positive attitude is far better than having a negative one.

I stay ahead of the game due to my positive attitude.

A positive attitude may not help me get everything, but it sure will get me a lot more than a negative attitude will.

<u>Action Items:</u>

1. Write down five things that you have achieved in the last 12 months largely because of your positive outlook and attitude.

2. Write down three things that you could have achieved and wanted to achieve but your negative attitude stopped you from doing so.

3. What can you do differently now to achieve those things that you couldn't before and to achieve more in the future?

Start With Gratitude

Take Care of Your Health

Have Written Goals

Your Attitude Determines Your Destiny

LESSON 4.

Have Written Goals

"Know where you want to go so that you can get there"

Of all the lessons you learn in this book, this undoubtedly is one of the top five. Goals are the guiding force for us. They are the fuel that fires us up to get more, do more, and become more in our chosen direction of life. We can, and we will, get someplace without goals, but the destination may not be the one we wanted.

Why written goals? Because writing them reinforces them in your mind; it also tells your subconscious that you are serious about them. Studies have proven again and again that those who have written goals achieve them more often and more quickly than those who never committed to them in writing. Write your goals and plans, and you will be pleasantly surprised with the results.

Since this book is about you setting your own destiny, it is absolutely important and crucial that you set goals and put them on paper. Also know that your goals will grow with you and sometimes, in different phases of your life, will take a completely different direction. So visit them often and change them as necessary to suit your needs and desires.

Goals are our road map. Without the map, it may take forever to get to our destination as we may take a much longer path. Also, without the road map, if we get lost, we will not turn back or change the direction as we will never find out that we are headed in the wrong direction. With the goals as our compass, we can move towards achieving our desired results with laser beam focus. Sure, there will be some diversions on our way, but we can fine tune and make adjustments to get to our known destination.

Think of an airplane pilot, headed from California to New York. He knows his destination without a shadow of the doubt. He knows how long it will take him to get there. And he also knows that there are conditions on the ground and in the sky completely beyond his control that could affect his flight plan. But one thing he knows for sure, and that is his destination. The plane departs from California on time, but on the way it encounters some rough weather patterns, so rough that an emergency landing is necessary in Pennsylvania. The pilot lands, waits for the weather to clear, and then continues to New York. The goal is clear—the plane must go to New York, and that is why it gets there instead of staying in Pennsylvania. This is how clear and concise each and every one of our goals should be. We must know how, when, where, and why we want to achieve our desired goals and we should be prepared for some distractions along the way.

Imagine a builder starting to build your home without any drawings or written plans? Without knowing the exact details of room sizes, construction materials, electrical and plumbing layouts, and many other facts? He wouldn't even consider beginning construction this way, and if he attempted to do so (and you let him do so), the project would be shut down by the township officials. And this is just for a home consisting of brick and mortar. If we can't even start a home without seeing the final product on paper first with all details in it, why then are we OK to run our lives without a written, detailed plan? And we wonder why we don't get the expected results! The least expensive things, even things like a one dollar plastic toy, come with manuals and directions to assemble and operate, the do's and don'ts, but our precious life does not. There is no manual that we must read to grow well in all phases of our life and perform at our very best. We must all establish our own path based on our experiences and the experiences of others, and by the time we get it, we have wasted many, many years of our life, sometimes beyond recovery (especially health issues). Perhaps each child should be given this book at the age of 9, so that they can use it as a manual for the rest of their life. What do you say?

Goals are normally divided into three categories—long term, mid term, and short term. Long term goals are usually 10-25 year goals; when life's purpose is clear, they can be lifelong goals. Mid-range goals normally range from 2-10 years. These goals are the stepping stones towards our long term goals. Short term goals are under two years; these are more for immediate needs and the baby steps for our mid-range and long term goals. Make sure you set your goals in all three of these categories.

The goals are best set if they start with the big picture in mind, your long term goals and desires. Steven Covey says, "Start with the end in mind." What if you are not sure or clear about those long term goals? Well, that's the beauty of putting things in writing. When you sit down to write them, you will develop clarity regarding your life's direction, your purpose, your mission. And that direction will free you of your worries of not knowing where you are headed. That's a huge reason why putting goals in writing is so critical.

The question I am often asked is, "What if my goals change mid-stream?" The answer is "That is okay!" It's better to move in a direction and then adjust it instead of having no direction at all. The second question I am often asked is, "Can we have multiple long term goals?" And the answer to that is yes, as long as they are not conflicting. You can't be in the army and be anti-violence at the same time.

One of your long terms goals will most likely lead you to your real purpose in life (we will discuss this in detail in another chapter), and at times your purpose in life will lead you to your long term goals.

When writing your goals, make sure they are well balanced. In fact, it is crucial that they are. Otherwise, you will pay a heavy penalty in one or more areas of your life while attaining success in another. Have written goals in the following five categories:

- Family goals
- Career goals
- Financial goals
- Health goals
- Spiritual goals

Working day and night to achieve your financial goals while ignoring your health is counterproductive. Very soon, you will have the wealth at the cost of your health. And then you will be giving away all your wealth later to get back your health. Makes no sense, does it? Not worth it, is it?

If written goals can guarantee our success many times more

than unwritten ones, why then, do many of us still not write them? There are a few possible reasons:

Reason Number One: We underestimate the power of written goals. We just haven't bought into their value and their possibilities.

Reason Number Two: We are stubborn (subconsciously). We think we will beat the odds and will prove to others that written goals are not necessary.

Reason Number Three: We are lazy. We procrastinate. We know the benefits but we keep putting it off till tomorrow. If you fall in this category, you should stop reading this chapter now and start writing your goals. Nothing beats just doing it.

Reason Number Four: Negative influence from others stops us from writing our goals. Some people have never written their goals down and are quick to tell you that it won't work for you. Don't share your goals with such people.

Reason Number Five: Past failures can stop you from putting your goals in writing. You have written them before but somehow never followed through, and now you don't believe they will work for you.

Reason Number Six: Fear of success, believe it or not, can be another reason. Some people are simply (subconsciously of course) afraid that if they put goals in writing, they may succeed and then lose all their friends and relatives who may not approve of their new status.

Reason Number Seven: Whatever your other reason is!

Regardless of your reason, put your goals in writing today! Do so now!

When writing your goals, make sure they are vivid, clear, specific, and have a time frame attached to them. Many people will tell you to make them realistic but I don't buy into the "realistic" theory. Wouldn't it be a shame to set realistic goals, achieve them, and then find out that you could have easily achieved much more if you would have stuck with your unrealistic goals? Go for unrealistic. Go for big. But be specific. Don't simply say 'I want to make a lot of money', as that is vague. Say, "I want to earn one million dollars next year by doing _____ _____ (whatever that is).

By the way, please make sure your goals are ethical, legal, and moral and that they don't hurt anyone in your quest to achieve them. Almost everything we need and want is available in abundance, so there is no reason to hurt anyone while trying to succeed.

One other thing on goals. Know that there is no FREE lunch. You will have to give something to get something in return. You need to work hard towards your goals and must have serious determination to achieve them. You cannot set a goal to triple your income next year while tripling your vacation time too. That's a conflicting goal under most circumstances. However it is not impossible if you have already paid a price for this in the last few years and everything is set to work that way. Or perhaps you have discovered a unique idea or product that will allow you to work hard and play hard at the same time.

Write your goals today. Review them daily, at least twice a day, and imprint them deep into your subconscious. Develop a burning desire to achieve your goals. Commit to achieving them despite any setbacks. Revise them in the future as necessary, and as often as necessary, in case your needs or desires change. I suggest that you carry them in your wallet or purse at all times. Stuck in traffic? Pull them out and read them. The wait is too long at the doctor's office? No problem, read your goals. Be prepared to achieve them much sooner than you ever imagined. You'll be pleasantly surprised as you often will!

One other thing! Please don't wait till December 31st to set your goals. Don't let a calendar date dictate your goal setting plan. Do it TODAY! Do it NOW!

"You can achieve your goals! You can and you will!"
All you have to do is have them in writing and then follow through as if your life depended on them.

Daily Affirmations:

My written goals are my road map.

I review my goals twice every day.

My daily actions are in tune with my written goals.

I am proud of my goals—they are legal, moral, and lofty.

Action Items:

1.   Write five, or more, long term goals (10 years or longer). Include all categories if possible. Be specific and vivid.

2.   Write five, or more, mid-range goals (two-10 years).

3. Write five, or more, short term goals (less than two years).

4. Now evaluate your short term and mid-range goals and see if they are helping you get to your long term goals. If not, you may want to revise them. If your long term goal is to be a cardiac surgeon, your mid-range goals cannot be completing your law degree.

5. Make a few copies of these goals. Put one in your wallet/purse, one at home and one in the office. Review and revise them often.

Start With Gratitude

Take Care of Your Health

Make Every Moment Count

Your Attitude Determines Your Destiny

Have Written Goals

LESSON 5.

Make Every Moment Count

"None of us is guaranteed our next moment. Make 'NOW' count."

God has granted every one of us 86,400 seconds a day. None of us, financially very rich or extremely poor, has a second less or a second more. The rich can't buy more time at any cost from anyone, and the poor can't sell time to any one at any cost.

So why is it that, given the same amount of time, some of us accomplish so much in a day while others do so little? Without a doubt, it is recognizing the value of time and proper planning. It's understanding that money can be lost and then made back, but time once lost is lost forever. There is no recovery process available for the lost time.

Once we understand this concept clearly, we give a whole new meaning to our time. We make sure that each second of ours is used for the right purpose, the purpose of our choice. Each second is well planned so that none of it is wasted. Each second goes towards meeting our goals and desires.

But can we plan each day of ours given that there are so

many interruptions all the time? The answer is absolutely YES. Anyone and everyone can plan their day as they choose to, with a back up contingency plan. In fact, it should be a crime not to. The only exception I can think of is when we are in a medical condition that has deprived us of our thinking capabilities. Then, in that case, someone else is planning our day. Otherwise, we can do so, even under the worst conditions and circumstances.

This planning of your day should be done with your goals in mind. What is your plan for your wealth, your family, your spiritual needs, and your career goals? Know that actions on some days will not fulfill all the categories and that is okay if that was part of your plan.

Have you ever heard colleagues or friends say "I don't know where my day went today"? That is a sign of an unplanned day. A well planned day will give you a sense of accomplishment knowing that you have achieved as desired. Even if there were deviations in the plan, you will still know that you did everything necessary to make the most of that day.

Results are almost never in our hands, but our actions towards achieving them are always controlled by us. When we take proper steps and actions, the desired results becomes more of a norm. Once you have done your best, leave the results to God. He knows what is best for you.

Does planning really give you more from your day? Let's think back. Let's think of the work day before your planned vacation/trip. How much more did you achieve on that day compared to your normal day? And why did you accomplish a lot more? Was it that your day all of a sudden became longer or was it because you took advantage of all the moments that would have been otherwise wasted had you not planned your day? Chances are you accomplished more on that day than on other days. And that is the beauty of planning. It lets you achieve a lot more with minimal mistakes. You get more out of each day when you plan it well. As an added bonus, you get more satisfaction from your work at a reduced stress level!

Each moment counts every day. Every moment in our life is precious; none of us is guaranteed the next one, so make each one count. Stop wasting your time watching silly TV shows or even worse, news commentary that is not even news, just someone's analysis of a hypothetical situation. Those moments can be well used for any of your five goal categories and will also give you a lot more pleasure in return, short term and long term.

Why is it that we are cautious before we waste/spend or donate money (something that can easily be made back) but are so careless in wasting time, which once spent can never be recovered? Perhaps we think we have unlimited time available to us. But the truth is our disposable time is limited at most. We should be wise spending ours and we should be careful not to waste someone else's.

When is the best time to plan your day? In my opinion, do it the night before or, if that is not possible on some days, plan it first thing in the morning. Know what you want to get out of your day. Plan to do the important things first and leave some flexible time for urgent tasks that may come up. The best way to plan a day is to put it in three categories.

Must Do—These things you must accomplish no matter what. Plan these as first things to be completed, if possible. These, in most cases, should be important things, not necessarily urgent things.

Have to Do—These may be your urgent things, things that if originally were planned might not have been as urgent but now need to be addressed nevertheless.

Want to Do—These are things you would like to do but are neither important nor urgent for that day.

In fact, there is one other category you should have:

Things Not to Do. This is huge as most of the time wasters will fall under this category. If you can avoid these things, your day will be much more productive.

Make each moment count. Respect the gift of time given to each one of us by our creator. Don't waste it; make the best use of it.

A bonus tip: Although you can't have more than 24 hours in any day, you can actually create extra hours, daily. How? Wake up at 4 a.m. instead of 7 a.m. You get 3 hours instantly. That is 21 hours a week, 1092 hours per year. Assuming a 7 hour work day, that comes to 156 extra work days a year, 31 extra work weeks, just by saving 3 hours daily.

"Why accept less, when more is possible?
You don't need more time in a day. You just need to get more out of your day by valuing each moment of yours, and others.

<u>Daily Affirmations:</u>

I plan each day in advance.

I do not waste any precious moments, mine or anyone else's.

I am fully satisfied with my planning of my time.

I make each moment count.

<u>Action Plan:</u>

I.   Create a To Do list divided in four categories:

Must Do:

Have to Do:

Want to Do:

Not to Do:

Make photocopies for daily use.

2. **Identify your daily time wasters and write solutions on how you can avoid them.** Examples could be sleeping too much, too much time on the internet, etc.

3. **Have a daily/weekly planner and plan each day the night before.**

Start With Gratitude

Take Care of Your Health

Your Attitude Determines Your Destiny

Improve Your Skills Constantly

Have Written Goals

Make Every Moment Count

LESSON 6.

Improve Your Skills Constantly

"We are either growing or dying, that is the law of nature."

What took centuries to change in the past now gets outdated in few years. The world is changing at a fast pace, and our knowledge of yesterday is not good enough for tomorrow's success. We must constantly be learning and upgrading our skills every day or we will be left way behind by those who are.

It used to be, not very many years ago, that large companies rarely laid off people. Once you got a job there, you were set for life. Not anymore. Now, everyone is replaceable in a heartbeat by someone who is more motivated, more skilled, and often willing to take a lower salary. And these replacements are not limited to borders of a country. Your replacement may come from any part of the world or your job may go to any part of the world. The internet has made the globe very small. Your replacement may be handled by a virtual assistant. Your replacement duties may be performed by a robot. The possibilities go on.

So how then, can we become irreplaceable? If we are let go by our company, how can we quickly find another job? The answer clearly lies in being a skilled employee/contractor who is current with today's needs and requirements. And that happens when you become a sponge for education and new skills. Not only do you need to stay updated in your job field, you also need to learn about other competitive fields, and study and practice personal growth in general. The more irreplaceable you become, the more you can demand for your skills. Give up the attitude of "I know it all already." That will sink you faster than anything else. Become someone who delivers more than is expected of them at a faster pace and with higher accuracy.

Being good is not good enough anymore. If you want to offer good results, you have to become very good. And if you want to produce great results, you have to become exceptional. Do not accept good when better is possible. Always aim towards being the very best for your own sake. And to be exceptionally best, you have to be a student everyday.

Read books, listen to tapes, attend seminars, and have a mentor/coach. Not only should you study the subject matter in your field of practice, you should also improve people skills, communication skills, and writing skills, among others. You may be the best in your field, but if you lack people skills, your growth potential is limited. Grow in all fields that you believe will help you excel. Know your strengths and weaknesses and then work on strengthening your strengths while you work on developing yourself to overcome your weaknesses. Know what you lack and then go seeking the ways to make up for those lacks.

Education is never a cost; it's an investment in yourself, and it pays back many times. If you believe the cost of education is high, then carefully evaluate the cost of ignorance. Look back and see how much more you could have been doing, or could have become, had you taken certain courses, and had you followed certain success tracks.

We all pay a price for lack of some skills/knowledge. Let us review salesperson Bob's performance and skill level and make some observations. Bob is an experienced salesperson. He is honest, and he puts his client's needs first. He knows his product very well. He has only one drawback—his closing skills are really weak. He makes a great presentation; the potential buyers get wowed by his knowledge and are ready to buy, but Bob never asks for an order. Because of this one lack, he loses many sales, each sale worth at least $2000. Bob's boss Bill realizes this drawback and suggests to Bob that he take a course on closing skills, the investment of which is $2500. This course, if taken, will help Bob immensely in making many additional sales and will far outweigh the investment in this course (yes, it's not a cost, it's an investment). Bob makes many excuses on why he doesn't need this course but the biggest one is that the course is too expensive. The question is, "Is this course really expensive?"

Chances are—in fact I can guarantee it—you said, "No, it is not expensive at all." If a $2500 investment can help increase the sales, with each sale worth at least $2000, how many sales does Bob need to make to recover his investment? Two at the most, and the rest is all gravy. Isn't that a great return on his investment? Sure it is!

Now here's the bigger question. Do you see yourself in Bob? Are you avoiding taking some courses even when you know that you need them and that the rewards will be worth it? Why did you say the course was not expensive when it came to Bob, yet when it comes to you, you are making the same excuses? You did, because it is easy to recognize the problems in others yet difficult to identify them within us. Don't pay such a penalty in your career. Improve your skills, and reward yourself well. In fact, make a commitment to improve yourself everyday, even if it is a little. Can't invest in a seminar? That's okay. Go to the library and borrow a book. Read the book and implement the suggestions given. The books are FREE in the library. It doesn't get better than that.

Do not leave to tomorrow what you can do today. Sign up for the course today. Get the book today. Watch your diet today. Do a little walking today. Don't leave things for a later date; they will start piling up. And some things just can't be compensated for anyhow. If you are supposed to take a multivitamin a day, you can't leave it for later and take 30 pills on one day, 30 days later. It just doesn't work that way, does it?

Improve your skills constantly, every day, even if the improvement is very little. Know that your future is in your hands. Know that for it to be, it is up to you.

"Become irreplaceable and become unstoppable."
No one can stop you from succeeding and achieving what your heart desires, except you.

Daily Affirmations:

I spend 30 minutes daily to improve my skills.

I am always looking for ways to enhance my value in today's fast changing world.

I don't accept good when better is possible for me.

Action Steps:

1. Evaluate your skills that need improvement. Be specific (e.g. I need to be a better public speaker so that I can be more effective in communicating my message).

2. Look for resources that will help you improve those skills.

3.   Sign up for at least one course immediately.

4.   Identify a book that can help you. Read it and then implement the lessons/ideas.

Start With Gratitude

Take Care of Your Health

Your Attitude Determines Your Destiny

Know Your Purpose

Have Written Goals

Make Every Moment Count

Improve Your Skills Constantly

LESSON 7.

Know Your Purpose

"Your purpose should not only inspire you, it should inspire others too"

Our true purpose in life is that ultimate desire to make a difference for the benefit of others and for the good of mankind. The real difference between a long term goal and a true purpose is simple —goals are self centered, purpose is all about others. Goals change often, purpose rarely changes.

There is nothing more rewarding than finding your purpose. And true purpose is always about selflessly serving others. It is closely connected to our spirituality and to our absolute belief and trust in God (Rama and Krishna in my case, but no matter what name we call Him by, the real trust in Him is what that matters). We are not human beings with a spiritual connection; we are spiritual beings temporarily in a human body. When we die, our human body dies but our spirit lives on. Our spirit had just taken on the body for this short stay. And it can leave this body whenever it chooses to.

Think of Mother Teresa's purpose. Think of Martin Luther King's purpose. Think of Mahatma Gandhi's purpose. Each had a purpose that was totally selfless. It was totally for the benefit of others. It was bigger than life. No wonder why they were so successful in fulfilling their purpose. Masses support you when your purpose is without any desire of personally benefiting from it.

So what is your purpose? What is that one thing you think of often and wish you could change for the benefit of many others, that one thing in whose pursuit you are willing to give up all you have? A purpose that excites you every time you think about it? A purpose that it totally non-selfish? A purpose that gives you energy beyond your imagination?

Let's look at some purposes out there—but please know that there are thousands and thousands more. You decide the one that you feel is right for you.

- Food for all so that there is no hungry person in a town/state/country.
- Medical treatment for every kid suffering from a specific disease (leukemia, blindness, etc).
- Education for each child in a town/state/country.
- Eradicating discrimination through education.
- Pollution free environment.
- Proper treatment and care for abused women.
- No cruelty towards animals.
- Spreading vegetarianism.
- Providing care for the elderly.

The list of purposes is unlimited. All you have to do is pick the one that gives you goose bumps. A purpose that deeply touches you, and resonates with your heart.

Once you find your purpose, all things will begin to fall in place. It will almost feel like a miracle. You will start wondering how that support is coming to you. Be prepared to welcome such support. Join hands with those who want to help and make it a reality.

Let me share my purpose with you! I want to reach out to poor children in India, and then in other parts of the world, to educate them, feed them and clothe them. To show them how to dream about their tomorrow. To help them connect with God. When this purpose became clear recently, my plan was to start with 200 kids, increase it to 500 in year two, and then double the numbers every year. But when the purpose is strong, these numbers, which look big in the beginning, look much smaller in time. Within months, my purpose expanded to touch one million kids in a 10-year span, starting from 2007 onwards. The goal will be to make each child self sufficient so that he/she can be part of this project and help other kids. Is it possible to really help so many kids in ten years? The answer is absolutely YES! When God shows you your purpose, He also provides the ways to fulfill it. We have to just make sure that there is no self motive in it, no desire to benefit personally from our purpose. If there is any possibility of a personal benefit, then this is not a purpose, it is a business!

Where will the money come for your cause? Don't worry about the money. In my case, I don't know that yet either except that all my books will be dedicated to a certain cause, with all proceeds going to that cause Also, one hundred percent of my speaking fees will go to serve my main purpose—the kids in India and abroad. And I know beyond a shadow of a doubt that the help will come from many who I have never even met or don't even know of yet. When the purpose is big, performed solely for the welfare of others with no greed for self, that purpose becomes the purpose of many, not just yours. Another possible gain from my true purpose is the lives I may touch through my books and seminars. Who knows who or how many will be inspired, who will then go on to serve a purpose that they can associate with? Wow, just the thought of this excites me and encourages me to keep writing on. I surely hope your purpose will do the same for you.

One last suggestion about your purpose: make sure the purpose is full of love. Make sure it is there to help others, not to hurt anyone. Be sure it is to give, not get. Hitler had a purpose, so did Saddam Hussein. Mother Teresa had a purpose, so did Mahatma Gandhi. Whom would you like to be associated with? How would you like to be remembered by your friends and family?

May you be inspired to find and fulfill a purpose bigger than life. May it grow beyond your own imagination. May God be with you in helping you with your purpose.

"When He gives you a purpose, He also gives you the means to accomplish it"
Have full faith in Him that HE is with you every step of the way, helping you help others.

Daily Affirmations:

My purpose (state it here) is bigger than me.

My purpose (state it here) is good for humanity.

My purpose (state it here) is unselfish and without greed.

Action Steps:

1. Search deep within you and find out what cause always gets your attention.

2. Analyze the cause and see if that can be your purpose. One way to tell is when you receive that inner feeling of excitement and content. A desire to say a loud 'YES' to that purpose.

3. Write how you will implement that purpose in your life and whose help you would need to accomplish that purpose.

Start With Gratitude

Take Care of Your Health

Your Attitude Determines Your Destiny

Have Written Goals

Give Up a Bad Habit

Make Every Moment Count

Improve Your Skills Constantly

Know Your Purpose

LESSON 8.

Give Up a Bad Habit

"One bad habit can easily wipe out all the goodwill one earned from all their great habits"

Imagine a glass filled with pure natural spring water. It's crystal clear, isn't it? Now add to it a drop of impurity, perhaps a drop of red ink. What happens to the water? It changes its color. The whole glass of pure water changed its color due to one drop of red ink. What if you were asked to drink the pure water with an explanation that the proportion of the ink compared to the whole glass of water is so minimal that it won't even matter? Would you drink it? What if you were told that the ink is non-toxic, would you drink it then? Probably not.

Our life works the same way too. We can have many good qualities and be proud of many great habits, but that one bad habit can sink us. That one habit can result in our downfall regardless of the good ones. That one habit can make us undesirable.

Do you have a habit that has been hard to give up? What has been the reason for not giving it up? Or perhaps you gave it up but then went back to it again. Are you convinced that it is such an addiction that you couldn't give it up even if you wanted to? Do you give your addiction so much importance that it has become bigger than you? That it carries much more significance than it's worth?

Rajnish, a well known Indian philosopher, gave a wonderful example of how we give significance to things just to avoid changing our habits. A man goes to his doctor complaining about cough and chest congestion. The doctor analyses the problem and asks the man to quit smoking. The man assures the doctor that he also wishes to quit smoking but he is afraid of the consequences if he quits. The doctor is surprised with the answer and asks for an explanation of his fears. The man replies "I quit smoking once. The day I quit smoking, World War II started."

This man really believed that the war started because he quit smoking and was afraid that if he did this again, another war would start! Wow, what a justification for not giving up a bad habit. This man was not worried about his real health and the consequences of it, but was giving an absurd amount of significance to a random coincidence. What an excuse to not give up smoking. However, he was so convinced that this became a valid reason for him to not quit.

Napoleon Hill says in his book *Think and Grow Rich,* "What a mind of man can conceive and believe, it can achieve." Sadly the mind of the man in the previous example conceived and believed a wrong thing, making himself a victim of that belief system. All results are caused by our belief system. Believe that you can give up a bad habit. See yourself already there. Enjoy the results permanently. And then just take steps to make that belief a realty.

Whatever your habit, please don't defend it. Recognize it and then take action.

Do you have a bad habit? And are you really serious about giving it up? Do you believe you can give it up? Do you make excuses as to why you can't or why you won't? Is that bad habit hurting you and your loved ones? The first step in giving up any bad habit is recognizing that it is bad. The second step is having a sincere desire to give it up. The third and final step is a belief system that you can give it up for good, for ever. If we miss any of these steps, the habit can't be broken; it is as simple as that.

Let's go back to smoking again. Many smokers don't even believe that smoking is bad. And if that's the case, how can they ever quit? In fact, I know of smokers who are proud to be the way they are and assure me that they would rather die then quit smoking or that everyone has to die so why should they not enjoy smoking (generally this happens when they are next to another smoker so they are showing off for the wrong reasons).

All the studies that prove the negative effects of smoking such as shortness of breath, lung cancer, etc. mean nothing to these smokers. The studies that show that second hand smoking hurts others (their spouse, kids, and friends) doesn't make them realize the danger. But if they don't believe that it is dangerous, then nothing else matters. The other two steps aren't even necessary.

Now let's say they believe that smoking is bad as they have seen a loved one suffer the consequences of smoking. Next comes the second step—a desire to quit. If their desire to smoke and socialize with those who smoke is stronger than their desire to quit, they can't give up that bad habit. They must sincerely desire to quit. It could be that they don't like the smell of smoke anymore. It could be that their kids have requested them to quit and now they have finally developed the desire to quit as well. Perhaps they have finally realized it's bad for their health (and for their wallet), and they have no desire to smoke anymore. The reason and desire to quit must be strong. This is the second necessary step.

And then the third and final crucial step. They must believe that they can quit smoking. Smokers blame it on addiction. They find many excuses that don't let them believe they can quit, and therefore they don't. And even if they do quit, they go back to smoking as soon as their belief system kicks in again saying that it is an addiction. To really quit, they must believe that they are stronger than any addiction or any other excuse.

Many a smoker has quit smoking permanently with these three components in place. So can everyone else. And so can you if that is a habit that you want to give up.

This three part process of giving up a habit can be applied to any bad habit that you may have. Follow the steps, and the habit will be gone. No, it won't be easy, but it is also not as difficult as many make it sound and believe.

Here are a few minor steps in addition to these three major ones. A stronger commitment, a bigger why (why do you want to quit, the real reason), and an open declaration of giving up the habit—all these can help a lot too. You can also set up a penalty for going back to the habit. Make that penalty huge so that you can feel the effect. It could be that you will donate $100 every time you smoke a cigarette, if you do at all. This amount may be much higher or lower based on your financial means, but a stretch nevertheless.

We are creatures of habits. And once a habit is formed, it takes effort and determination to break it. Best is not to let a bad habit start anyhow. Smoking, drinking, overeating, stealing, lying—these are all bad habits. Sometimes, you may just involuntarily think of going to your bad habit. In that case you can have some reminders that will create a little pain (yet memorable). You could pinch yourself, gently slap yourself, bite your tongue, etc. This can be an excellent reminder and help you with your will power to achieve desired results.

Just as you can punish yourself for going back to your habit, you should reward yourself for your good actions too. How about setting a reward for giving up your habit—something you would otherwise not give to yourself. Decide on a reward, and when the habit is gone, reward yourself without any excuses. The reward could be monetary, it could be in the form of travel, or it could be anything you choose it to be. Remember, this reward is about you, for you.

Getting rid of a habit is a goal. Follow the guidelines on goal setting and free yourself from your bad habit(s). I wish you the best in identifying your bad habits and then following these simple yet not necessarily easy skills to give up those habits forever. I would love to hear your success stories as well as what worked for you. May God be with you in helping you succeed! He always is!

"Small actions lead into permanent habits."
Be careful of your actions. Recognize the consequnces.

Daily Affirmations:
I control my actions; no habit is stronger than my will-power.

I choose to give up (state your bad habits here):

I set an example for others by showing them that any habit can be given up at will.

Action Plans:

I.   Identify your bad habits. Habits that might be caus-ing you or others physical, financial, emotional, or other hurts.

2. Write in detail these identified hurts. An example could be, "I smoke a pack a day: it's costing me $6/day, $40/week, $2000/year, and if I saved so much annually, I could be worth millions in just 30 years. It is also hurting me physically as I am short of breath due to smoke. I am also not setting a good example for my kids. I feel bad that I rely so strongly on this habit to make me feel better." More the detail, better the results.

3. Write the pleasures/ benefits you will gain by giving up the bad habit.

4. Give up the bad habit immediately. Set a penalty and reward system.

Start With Gratitude

Take Care of Your Health

Your Attitude Determines Your Destiny

Have Written Goals

Take Action

Make Every Moment Count

Improve Your Skills Constantly

Know Your Purpose

Give Up a Bad Habit

LESSON 9.

Take Action

"All planning is worthless if it is not followed through with action."

Of all the lessons in this book, this is perhaps one of the most important as here the rubber meets the road. All of our good intentions mean nothing if we don't take action and turn those intentions/commitments into a reality. Nothing happens till we act. Although dreaming and planning are important and very necessary, it's the action that makes them a reality. No action means no results, it is as simple as that.

Imagine having a vision to build the tallest building in the world. You find the right site. You go and hire an architect and an engineer. You do all the planning. But you never start building. What good are the plans if the building is never started and completed? Planning is absolutely essential, but the vision only comes true if you take action and build the place.

Knowing that you should thank God for your blessings everyday is good, but actually thanking is what counts. Knowing that eating an apple a day is good, but eating the apple is what matters. Knowing your purpose is great, but acting to make it a reality is a must. Knowing that walking is good for your health is important. Buying the right walking shoes is important. But only actual walking will give you the benefits of walking. What we say and believe means nothing unless we act on it. Preparation is important, action is a MUST. You get the point, right?

So what stops people from taking action? There are many reasons and some of them are:

Our old habits—Procrastination, oversleeping, wasting time or not valuing time; these and many more such habits result in lack of time for taking action.

Not appreciating the true benefits—Unless the benefit of our action outweighs our old habit conditioning, we will not have the real desire to take action. Remind yourself of the benefits you will enjoy when you act. Know what difference you will make, and to whom and how, when you take the action. See yourself already there.

Fear of failing—This fear stops many. They are afraid of failing and feel it is safer not to even start. They buy into the comments of critics, and even their well meaning friends, who advise them to be cautious and slow. They don't want their friends telling them later, "We told you so."

Lack of knowledge—This is not as big of a reason in today's world where answers to almost anything are available at the click of the mouse, but some people just don't know where to start.

Being Perfect—Yes, this can be a big reason for not taking action. We want to be sure that the project is perfect or foolproof, and therefore keep putting it off till that 100% assurance sets in.

Whatever your reason for not taking action, analyze it, and

then proceed. Be prepared for the worst and expect nothing but the best. Once we are prepared for the worst, nothing can stop us from taking action. Know that the actions are in your hands, even if the results are not. So take the action, do your very best to reach your desired result, and then leave the result to God. Accept His will, whether it works your way or not!

When breaking a habit of any kind, know that it takes 21 days of deliberate action to break that habit. Some habits can be broken by taking baby step actions, others may need massive actions. To create any new habit, an old habit needs to be destroyed. Say you want to create a habit of walking daily for three miles a day. The new habit is walking; the old habit is laziness, too much sleep, lack of time, or something else. You decide which old habit it stopping you from walking. Let's say it is lack of time. Your first step then, is to make time. Can you wake up early? Can you stop wasting time on unnecessary things such as watching TV, reading newspapers etc., and use it for walking? Can you go for a walk during your lunch hour? Once the time is found, walk a mile for the first few days. Then increase it to two miles, and in the third week start walking three miles. Baby steps will help you get to three miles a day in no time.

Never leave the crucial steps of taking an action to tomorrow. Do something today, do something now that leads you to the main action tomorrow. Let's say you want to attend a seminar that you just heard of. But it's late in the evening and you can't call to register. What other choices do you have? Can you e-mail them? Can you leave a message on the machine? How about just writing this in your To Do list for tomorrow? This small action of writing down will build momentum to take the action of registration tomorrow. Take an action today, no matter how small it is.

At the end of each lesson in this book, we have affirmations and an action plan. Have you said your affirmations? Have you acted on those action plans? Or have you just enjoyed reading the book but have no interest in taking any actions? The results come from actions. The stronger your actions are, the stronger your results will be. And for permanent results, you need continued strong actions.

You have probably heard of "Ready, Aim, Fire." This is a great thing if we do all three. The problem with most of us is that we get ready and we aim, but we never fire till we are sure of our aim. Don't make that mistake. It is okay to miss sometimes, or for that matter, many times. Fire often. And when you find that you missed your target, re-aim and fire again. Action is the key if you want to hit your target. Nothing is sure or guaranteed in life except one thing—you will never make it to the end if you don't start.

Our dreams, our goals, and our plans have no meaning unless we take action. Don't die with your dream in you. Don't let your dreams/goals meet you at your deathbed, in the form of angels, and curse you for killing them along with you. Have faith in yourself. Give life to your dreams and goals. Move forward through action.

"Take action everyday, no matter how small!"
All fruits we enjoy today are results of our past sown seeds. Sow for your future, today and everyday.

Daily Affirmations:

I take daily actions towards my goals.

I know that nothing gets accomplished without action.

All my achievements are due to the actions I have taken in the past.

All my dreams come true through my actions.

Action Plan:
Do it TODAY, Take Action now.

1. Write down all things important to you, things that you have been wanting to do but haven't done.

2. What has been stopping you from getting those things done?

3. What actions can you take today, even if very small, to get those things jump started?

Start With Gratitude

Take Care of Your Health

Your Attitude Determines Your Destiny

Have Written Goals

Make Every Moment Count

Have Patience

Improve Your Skills Constantly

Know Your Purpose

Give Up a Bad Habit

Take Action

LESSON 10.

Have Patience

"All actions are wasted when the proper amount of patience is not applied."

Isn't it ironic that you read about taking action in the last lesson, and now I tell you to be patient? Yup, this was planned that way.

Many people take action but have no patience to wait for results. In today's world of instant gratification, even instant is not fast enough. In fact, we expect results even before we take action. And that sets us up for failure. If the results are not obvious quickly, we quit. But we must remember that patience is a virtue. All good things take time.

We must take action, but we must be patient with the results. Imagine a farmer sowing seeds and then expecting the crop the very next day? Yet that is how most of us live. We want our crop the next day. But not the farmer. The farmer prepares the soil and then takes the action of planting the seed. He waters the ground and fertilizes the soil. He removes the weeds often. And then he waits for the nature to take its course. The farmer knows that his actions are absolutely important, but he also knows that the nature will play its role and that the plant will bear fruit in due time.

The farmer knows that it will take time for the plant to mature as desired. The farmer knows that he has to wait for the right season for his crop to grow. He has to be fully patient; he has no other choice. His actions were absolutely important in getting the plant started, but his patience is even more important once his part is done.

We too must follow the laws of nature. We must do our part, the very best we can, and then wait patiently for the desired results. Some crops come in a season, some take a few, and some take years. The bigger the plant, the longer the time expected. Small plants come sooner but last only for a season or two and have to be reseeded again next year. Big trees take years to grow, but then they give fruits year after year.

Some monkeys once got together and decided they no longer wanted to be dependent on their keeper for food. They decided to grow some banana trees for themselves. They all worked together and sowed the proper seeds in the ground. Action was prompt on their part. Then, they all sat on the ground, waiting for the tree to pop up. Pretty soon they started getting impatient. They just couldn't figure out why it was taking so long. So they all decided to dig the ground again to see if the germination had started and if the roots were formed yet. Their lack of patience messed up all their efforts and actions. Funny we laugh at these monkeys, yet many of us are like that. We don't have the patience to give the needed time for the real results. We want to be rich overnight. We want our business to grow overnight. We want to reach our goal instantly. And when this doesn't happen, we give up! We start changing out plans. We invent new ways without giving time for old ones to work. We start a walking program, don't see the benefit right away, and quit walking. We start eating healthy food, don't lose the weight in a few days, and go back to our regular eating. Aren't we just like these monkeys, messing ourselves up due to lack of patience?

Next time you take on a project and take all actions to achieve the results, remember to be patient. Know that you need to give the necessary time for achievement of the desired result. Have faith in your actions, and then have patience in getting your results. Do this and the success will surely be yours. Remember the lessons learned from the farmer:

1. The farmer knows the end result very clearly. He knows that he wants corn to grow in his field.
2. He has the knowledge of the process. He knows what kind of seeds to use, what kind of soil and fertilizer, how much spacing between seeds, how much watering, etc, etc.
3. He takes action and plants the right seeds. He wants corn, he plants corn seeds. He doesn't plant tomatoes and expect corn.
4. He takes daily action as needed to cultivate the crop. He just doesn't sow the seeds and expect corn in a few months.
5. He waits patiently for his crops. He knows that this is not an instant process. He also knows that if he gives up in between, all efforts thus far will go wasted and he will have to start all over again. He is also prepared to depend on nature and know that nature may not cooperate. He knows that his failure to get crops won't

be his doing, and he gladly accepts this. He knows that if it doesn't happen this year, he has next year and then the next.

6. He is prepared for the worst but hopes for the best through his actions and patience.

7. He has faith in the process and in God. He knows how it has worked for others for centuries, and he has faith that it will work the same way for him.

8. He harvests his crop when it is ready. He doesn't take off during the harvest time.

Miss any of the steps, and the farmer is doomed to fail. See yourself as a farmer of your dreams. Don't miss any steps when working on your goals or your purpose.

Once action is taken, patience becomes the key to success of any project. Give the project the time it needs. What took years to do (e.g. gaining weight) can't be and shouldn't be expected to be lost in a day. Take daily actions and have patience.

Next time when you catch yourself getting impatient with anything, recognize it. Start with small things. It could be as simple as your meal taking a little longer at the restaurant or perhaps the driver ahead of you driving slower than you would want him to. You may be in a rush in both cases, but tell yourself to be patient. Small things add up to big things. This practice to be patient in small things will help you when it comes to more important projects.

May God bless you with the patience necessary to see your actions become fruitful.

"Put your best foot forward and then simply wait"

Always remember the farmer when you become impatient for results.

Daily Affirmations:
I take necessary actions and am patient with the results.

I am patient as I have faith in God's plans for me.

I resolve to be patient with small things so that I can be patient with big things.

Action Items:

1. What projects have you taken on and then given up half way through because of lack of patience?

2. Do you believe that you can revive some of those by being more patient?
    Would you like to give them another try? If so, go for them.

3. Add the conscious decision of being patient - with all your goals and with regard to your purpose in life, once you have taken actions. Know that God is with you, and that the results will be according to His will.

BONUS LESSONS

Lessons 11 thru 20

The bonus lessons are not elaborated in detail and come without daily affirmations and action plans. I want you to get more involved in these chapters and make this book really yours! I suggest that you read each lesson and then write your affirmations and action plans based on your understanding of the lesson.

I would love to hear from you regarding what you wrote for affirmations and action plans! Please email me your comments and thoughts at sanjeev@sanjeevaneja.com

Start With Gratitude

Take Care of Your Health

Your Attitude Determines Your Destiny

Have Written Goals

Make Every Moment Count

Do What is Right

Improve Your Skills Constantly

Know Your Purpose

Give Up a Bad Habit

Take Action

Have Patience

LESSON 11.

Do What is Right

"There is no wrong time to do what it right"

Always do what is right. Don't base your decisions on the popularity of the masses. Don't compromise your values to please others. Do things that are principle- based, not popular-ity-based, regardless of the consequences. What's popular today will change tomorrow, but principle-based decisions will last forever.

How can you tell if something is right or wrong? Almost every time, your inner self will give you the right answer. All you have to do is ask yourself for internal guidance. Here are a few questions that will help you differentiate between the right and the wrong.

Question One: Is my action going to harm anyone else?

Question Two: Is my action going to harm me physically, emotionally, or spiritually?

Question Three: Is my action going to help others in a positive way?

Question Four: Is my action going to help me in a positive way?

Question Five: Can I openly and proudly tell others about my action?

Question Six: Will it be necessary for me to hide my action from my loved ones or anyone, for that matter?

If the answers to these questions are clear and you are satisfied with them, then the action is right. If answers to these questions come with a question, then the action needs to be reconsidered.

Let's review this through a quick example. Say you have never smoked before, and one of your friends asks you to try smoking. Should you smoke? Is your action right? Let's ask the questions and determine the right answer.

Q: Is my action going to harm anyone?
A: It may. Isn't second hand smoking harmful to others?

Notice, we don't even have to go to the second question. We can stop right here. The answer had a maybe in it, and had a question in it too, so our answer is clear. But let's try the next question anyhow.

Q: Is my action going to harm me?
A: Absolutely yes. Smoking is not good for my health.

Your answer/decision now becomes crystal clear. You shouldn't start smoking.

"Popular doesn't make it right. Right makes it right."
Always do what is right. Don't be pressured by anyone to do what is wrong.

Daily Affirmations:

1.

2.

3.

Action Plans:

1.

2.

3.

Start With Gratitude

Take Care of Your Health

Your Attitude Determines Your Destiny

Have Written Goals

Make Every Moment Count

Improve Your Skills Constantly

Your Past is not Equal to Your Future

Know Your Purpose

Give Up a Bad Habit

Take Action

Have Patience

Do What is Right

LESSON 12.

Your Past is not Equal to Your Future

"One can't drive successfully while looking in their rear view mirror."

Many lives are ruined because people get stuck in their past hurts. Many a success is left unachieved because people can't get over their past failures.

As much as we wish and want to do what is right, mistakes are a part of our growth. They will happen, knowingly and unknowingly. Some things we know are wrong. Others, only the future can tell, as the intentions in the moment they were taken were totally right.

Whatever the reason, make your past experiences, good or bad, a stepping stone for your bright future. If the experience was good for you and your loved ones, and it didn't hurt anyone in the process, build on it and make it even better. If the results were not as you would have wished, then learn from those mistakes and become a better person. Get past your errors in judgment. Don't mess up your future and that of your loved ones by drowning yourself in sorrow and making yourself feel less worthy. Forget the pity party. Remember all your past successes and good deeds and then compare your mistakes with them. Give yourself credit for all the good you have done in the past and the victories you have achieved.

Your failure yesterday has nothing to do with your actions today. If you fail, for whatever reason, you must quickly recover. Don't get hung up in playing the blame game. Fall, and bounce back quickly. Be like that one year old. When she falls, she doesn't stay in that position for any longer than necessary. She gets up immediately and tries again, and again, and again. And what do we do as parents when we watch her fall? We encourage her to get up. And she does. Imagine the child saying, "I fall often, I can't do this." No, no, no, that doesn't even cross her mind unless someone tells her that she can't and she unfortunately believes that someone. What a shame would that be! Also, as parents, imagine us telling the child that she should now give up, as she has fallen few times and it is not worth trying! We'd never do that, would we? We know in our mind, without the shadow of a doubt, that the child will walk. Sadly, as adults, we have many people in our life that will remind us often about our falls and will discourage us from standing up. Refuse to listen to those people. Stand up quickly, and start running immediately.

What if you start a business and it fails? Would you give up? No, you MUST NOT. Learn from the mistakes and try again and then try again, but try you must. Your past is not equal to your future. Success will come; it has to. The same thing applies to your health, your relationships, your spirituality. Learn lessons from the past and make your future a bright one. A future that is not only worth it for you, but for all your loved ones, and for all those who need your help.

"Fools blame their present on their past, wise learn from
their past and make their future bright."

Do not let your past mess up your future.

Daily Affirmations:

1.

2.

3.

Action Plans:

1.

2.

3.

Start With Gratitude

Take Care of Your Health

Your Attitude Determines Your Destiny

Have Written Goals

Make Every Moment Count

Improve Your Skills Constantly

This Too Shall Pass

Know Your Purpose

Give Up a Bad Habit

Take Action

Have Patience

Do What is Right

Your Past is not Equal to Your Future

LESSON 13.

This Too Shall Pass

"All things are temporary. Nothing is permanent."

Have you experienced a day or days when everything you attempted went wrong (or it at least appeared that way at that moment)? You had good intentions, you were trying your hardest and your best, it had worked in the past like clockwork, but that day, somehow it just wouldn't? Here's the good news. It happens to all of us. We all have such days. What matters the most is our reaction to such events. Will we flip out or will we handle the event calmly? Will we give up or will we keep trying? Will we blame others for such results or will we look within to grow from it? Will we react to the situation or respond to it? When you take medication to heal you from an illness, the right medicine helps your system respond to it, not react to it! Similarly, you need to respond in the times of a problem, not react.

No situation in life is permanent. That's the law of nature. Day must follow night and vice versa. Winter must follow fall, which must follow summer; we can't change it. It's not permanent, nothing is. Neither is our tough situation. In its moment, when it happens, it may seem like something that you will never get past. But your full understanding and belief that this situation is very temporary will give you the calmness you need to know that this is not a big deal. Most things are forgotten moments later, if we choose to forget them. It's not the things that happen; it's the meaning/importance we give to the situation that matters.

I personally have a note, 'THIS TOO SHALL PASS,' posted on my office wall. Why? Just as a reminder for those tough moments—and for those great moments too. Just as we shouldn't be messed up due to what is going wrong, we shouldn't get too comfortable when all is going right. Being humble and having humility are very important; we need to remember that good times can change instantly, too. Acting in a manner inconsistent with how any good human being should only hurts us in the future. Know that all situations are temporary.

Regarding tough times, here are a few suggestions:

1. Do not call your problem a problem. Call it a challenge. Problems weigh us down.
2. Say it loud to yourself, "This too shall pass."
3. Look at your challenge as if it is not happening to you but to someone else on the other side of the world. When you do that, your challenge will look much smaller, as you are not directly associated with it anymore. You are now helping someone else. You will be able to find a solution for that someone, as you have temporarily brought yourself out of that situation. And that solution for them now becomes your solution. See how it works? See how simple it is?
4. The last step is to take some immediate action, no matter what it is. Let's say you just lost your job (or that other person lost the job). Your advice would be to prepare a resume, call credit card companies to request delayed payments, etc.

Now take that advice and implement it immediately. It's never the loss of a job that is a problem; it is a fear of our tomorrow that worries us. It's our committed expenses that worry us It's the fear of the unknown that scares us. Once you take action towards eliminating those concerns, it all works out and looks pretty simple, actually.

Yes, a real situation is a concern, no doubt about it, but how we respond makes all the difference. We can be sad, go to a bar and have a lot of drinks to forget our pain (a reaction) or we can get our resume ready and send it to a few companies (a response). Same situation, different results. It is all up to us.

**"Responding to your situation is always a better,
well thought of choice"**
Know that This Too Shall Pass. It has to.

Daily Affirmations:

1.

2.

3.

Action Plans:

1.

2.

3.

Start With Gratitude

Take Care of Your Health

Your Attitude Determines Your Destiny

Have Written Goals

Make Every Moment Count

Improve Your Skills Constantly

Know Your Purpose

Laugh it off

Give Up a Bad Habit

Take Action

Have Patience

Do What is Right

Your Past is not Equal to Your Future

This Too Shall Pass

LESSON 14.

Laugh it off

"Don't hang on to your setback when you can easily get rid of it."

"Laugh it off" is the other note that I have hanging on my wall.

No matter how much of a positive thinker we are, a time will come when things don't look right and we almost want to scream and cry. But not you. You know that the response is in your hands and that you have choices. You can simply laugh it off. Know it will pass, and laugh at the situation you are in. Please know that making such a choice at that moment of stress is not going to be easy. But also know that it is a better choice for you compared to any other available.

There are many things in life that we have no control over. An employee had a bad day and now they want to ruin yours (unknowingly); an unsafe driver cuts you off and you get into an accident because of it; you lock your keys in your car just when you have to get to a very important meeting. Things will happen. That's life. You can't always control such events. But you can control your actions. You are not ordinary, you are different. While others cry, yell and scream over such things, you simply laugh it off. Let me assure you again that it is not going to be easy to laugh when such a situation happens. Everyone's first inclination is to get upset; we have been programmed like that all our lives. But not anymore; you are simply not going to ruin your day for this. If you must get upset, do so and then get over it instantly. Start laughing at the situation (not very loud though, because those who haven't read this book may think you are crazy). Give a different meaning to the event, and it will feel different. Your thoughts can change your outcome instantly. Let's see how.

Say you were cut off by a crazy driver. He sped off, he is gone, but you get into a fender bender because of his mistake. The situation can't change anymore; it is what it is. But here are two different reactions (in fact a reaction and a response):

Reaction: You curse that driver. You kick your car. You cry. You get upset. You speed up to catch up with that driver and hit someone else in your anger. In fact, this is what most people do. But not you.

Response: You sympathize with that driver. You wonder if he had a sick family member in the car who was dying and he was rushing them to the hospital. Or, perhaps he was rushing home because his three-year-old was really sick. You pray for that guy. You thank God that you didn't get into a bigger accident. You thank God that you are not in this person's shoes. You thank God and acknowledge that everything happens for a good reason. You stay calm and collected.

The situation was the same, right? But how about the internal results? Which was more powerful for you, the reaction or the response? Reaction created anger and anxiety. Response created sympathy for the other driver and a sense of calmness and gratitude within you. Which would you prefer, anyhow?

"When the going gets tough, the tough get going."
Don't make any situation bigger than it is! Laugh it off!

Daily Affirmations:

1.

2.

3.

Action Plans:

1.

2.

3.

Start With Gratitude

Take Care of Your Health

Your Attitude Determines Your Destiny

Have Written Goals

Make Every Moment Count

Improve Your Skills Constantly

Know Your Purpose

Do What You Love, Love What You Do

Give Up a Bad Habit

Take Action

Have Patience

Do What is Right

Your Past is not Equal to Your Future

This Too Shall Pass

Laugh it off

LESSON 15.

Do What You Love, Love What You Do

"Your quality of work is reflected in your love for the work."

Life is short. Why then should we do what we don't love? Why then should we not love what we do?

When we love what we do, the quality of our work reflects in the work. The pride in our performance is obvious. It doesn't feel like work, it feels like play. Our work is error-less (or close to it). Our work is exemplary. We look forward to going to work everyday. There is no stress whatsoever.

When we don't love what we do, it is just the opposite. There are mistakes all over. Life is stressful. We dread going to work and complain when getting out of bed. We are often sick.

Whenever possible, turn your hobby into your work. If you love gardening, find work in that field. If you love building planes, then become an aeronautical engineer. Your love and passion for things will take you a lot further than a compromise. Look at any successful entrepreneur, and you will see that they loved their work first, and then they became successful. They didn't become successful because of their work; their work made them successful because of their love for it.

Although it is possible for many of us to follow our dream and do what we love, most of us don't. It could be because our education was in a different field, it could be because our current job is paying well, and it could be many other reasons. And we are always complaining about something or the other because our heart is not in what we do. Here is where the choices come in. You have a choice to stay miserable at your current job and get nowhere in life; you have a choice to start loving your current job (love the salary, the benefits, the comfortable environment) and reflect the same in your performance thereof; and you have a choice to leave your current job and follow your heart to a job that you love. Which one do you choose? I hope, for your own sake, you don't select the first one. You are doing yourself a huge disservice by staying where you are and being miserable. Either love it and give it your best or get out of it and do what you love to do so that you can perform at your best.

If you don't want to change jobs, then start loving your work. How can you start loving your current job? How can you change your attitude towards what you do? Find things that you like about having a job—salary, friends, vacations, opportunities to serve others, opportunities to get away from home, and much more. Start loving your job (even if you have to fake it), and then see the quality of your performance improve many fold. When your performance goes up, you will be recognized for the same. When that happens, you will love your job more, and the process continues. It all starts with you loving what you do. Our love for work reflects the quality of our work without a shadow of the doubt. Be proud to sign off on what you do, regardless of how much you get paid. Do that, and watch yourself climb the ladder of success. The ladder starts at $8/hour, but it has no to limit to where it ends. Your success and your future depend solely on you. All you have to do is put your heart into it. Then, your work will not feel like work. You will actually enjoy getting out of bed and getting to your work. Know that you must perform first and show your worth first before you can expect to be put on the ladder of success.

"Change your attitude towards your work or change your work"

Many people go to their jobs daily as if someone had pushed them into it. Let your job pull you towards it.

Daily Affirmations:

1.

2.

3.

Action Plans:

1.

2.

FOR IT TO BE, IT'S UP TO ME

3.

Start With Gratitude

Take Care of Your Health

Your Attitude Determines Your Destiny

Have Written Goals

Make Every Moment Count

Improve Your Skills Constantly

Know Your Purpose

Give Up a Bad Habit

Be a Positive Thinker

Take Action

Have Patience

Do What is Right

Your Past is not Equal to Your Future

This Too Shall Pass

Laugh it off

Do What You Love, Love What You Do

LESSON 16.

Be a Positive Thinker

"You have to think anyway, why not think positive?"

Our thoughts are very powerful. Thoughts are like seeds: when we sow negative thoughts, we get negative results; and when we sow positive thoughts, out come the positive results. As we sow, so shall we reap.

Negative thoughts are like weeds. We don't even have to sow them. They grow automatically and have to be weeded out. Positive thoughts, on the other hand, must be planted. And they must be planted everyday. And they must be sown with absolute faith in God and a belief that they will bring positive results.

Whatever your situation, look for good in it. Look for lessons you want to learn from it. Be like the fourth grader who was playing baseball all by himself. He threw the ball up in the air, shouted out loud that he was the best hitter in the world, swung the bat, and missed the ball. He attempted again, repeated his affirmation of being the best batter, but missed the ball again. He went again and couldn't hit the third time either. Without missing a beat, he shouted out loud, "I am the best pitcher." He couldn't hit the ball, but that was not going to stop him from finding the good. He quickly turned the negative into positive.

Always expect positive results. Always see the glass half full instead of the glass half empty. Always be thankful for what you have instead of complaining about what you don't. Always be thankful for your blessings. Just this little change in your outlook of things will bring wonderful results in your life.

Whenever a negative thought comes to your mind, replace it with a positive one. It won't be easy in the beginning, but practice makes perfect. All you have to do is recognize your thoughts and correct them. And how do we differentiate between negative and positive? The BEST way to do so is to feel your energy level at that moment. Negative thoughts drain your energy, and positive thoughts give you energy. When a thought enters your mind, feel your physical energy.

The company we keep makes a big difference. Being part of a group where thoughts are about hate and hurt makes the energy level stay very low. Be part of a loving and giving group, and the energy level changes dramatically. Many tests have proven the enormous value of our thoughts over and over again. But we don't need to review any studies; this can be experienced by us first hand whenever we choose to do so.

Keep your thoughts in control. Work as hard as you can to keep them positive and constructive. Your thoughts mean EVERYTHING! You are where you are in life because of your thought process.

"Sow positive thoughts. Get positive results."
Never let any well meaning friend tell you it is okay to have negative thoughts.

Daily Affirmations:

1.

2.

3.

Action Plans:

1.

2.

3.

Start With Gratitude

Take Care of Your Health

Your Attitude Determines Your Destiny

Have Written Goals

Make Every Moment Count

Improve Your Skills Constantly

Know Your Purpose

Give Up a Bad Habit

Have Faith in Yourself

Take Action

Have Patience

Do What is Right

Your Past is not Equal to Your Future

This Too Shall Pass

Laugh it off

Do What You Love, Love What You Do

Be a Positive Thinker

LESSON 13.

Have Faith in Yourself

"Nothing great is possible, unless one has faith in it"

True faith is that absolute assurance in which no doubt exists. It is faith of that two year old daughter in her dad that she jumps off a chair and expects her dad to catch her in his arms. It is our faith in nature, and in God, that assures us that the day will come after the night, that one season will follow the other, that a seed will change into a plant. It is our faith in the pilot when we fly that sees us through our destination. And it is our faith in so many other things that adds calm and certainty to life.

Fear is the opposite of faith. Although some fear is necessary to avoid chaos, too much fear is what robs us of our potential. It is fear that stops us from trying new things and following our dreams. And that is where faith comes in. When you have faith in yourself and your creator, almost everything is possible. When you have absolute faith, you are unstoppable. Everything is possible for those who believe in Him and, in turn, themselves.

Faith is like a candle, while fear is like a dark room. Light a candle in a dark room and the darkness instantly disappears. Bring in faith when you are afraid, and the fear will be gone.

Fear can not exist when faith is around. The stronger your faith, the weaker your fear. Master your faith, and you will conquer your fear.

Your utmost faith starts with trust in God. That's an absolute must—your truest strength in your weakest moments. And after that comes your faith in you. Regardless of your situation, your faith in yourself and your capabilities determines your end result. Anything done without that faith and anything done with doubts, especially a doubt in yourself, can not produce the very best result.

Nothing is impossible for those who have faith in God and in themselves. If He has given you an idea (your seed), He has done so because He knows that you can make it a reality. All you have to do is trust yourself and take action, and leave the results to Him.

Why is it that we have faith in other people's capabilities but not our own? Why is that we have faith in mechanical components, such as a car, but little faith in our priceless mind and body? Why do we live a lesser life than we can and are capable of? Why? Because we have not developed our faith in ourselves. We have bought into other people's garbage of what we can do and what we can't, perhaps subconsciously, from our young age. And the only way to break that belief is by going out of our comfort zone and doing what we think we can't do.

Look back at your life in the last 10-15 years. What has stopped you from becoming or achieving what you wanted to? Whose wrong belief system have you bought into? What is your level of faith in yourself, and why is it that low? If you failed in the past, did you try again, and then again, and then again? What would have been the results today had you tried and achieved those dreams? Was lack of faith worth the penalty of not achieving your desired goals? Although we can't do much about the past missed opportunities, except learning lessons from them, we can develop our faith in us going forward. You don't want to be doing this analysis 15 years from now and finding the same pattern in your results, do you?

Start building your faith in yourself beginning today. If you already have it, that is great. Now kick it up a notch. You are capable of more than you already are. And you probably know that too.

Faith lets us do things that otherwise are not possible. Faith lets us achieve milestones that might have not otherwise even been attempted. Faith leads us to possibilities. Faith leads us to true results.

Our biggest regrets in life are not things that we have attempted and failed in; instead, they are things that were all possible for us but we never even tried, perhaps due to lack of faith in ourselves. But it is never too late for most things. We are often heard saying, "I wish I had done this when I was younger." While we can't go back in time, we can stop talking about what is gone and start working today on our tomorrow. Have faith that you can do it. Become unstoppable. Do what your heart desires, as long as it is moral, ethical, and doesn't hurt anyone in the process. Go for it!

Thinking of starting a business? A charitable foundation?

Taking dance classes? Running for an office? Whatever it is, do it. And do it with absolute faith, knowing that you can. Put all your trust in yourself and in God. Know that when you have given your all with absolute faith, God will make it happen for you. And if it doesn't happen for whatever reason, know that He knows what is right for you. Absolute faith is the key.

You can do anything you choose to. Keep your faith alive and go do it! God is with you!

"Faith is the key ingredient that makes success possible"
Without faith, one doesn't even start anything. And if we don't start it, how can we see it through?

Daily Affirmations:

1.

2.

3.

Action Plans:

1.

2.

3.

Start With Gratitude

Take Care of Your Health

Your Attitude Determines Your Destiny

Have Written Goals

Make Every Moment Count

Improve Your Skills Constantly

Know Your Purpose

Give Up a Bad Habit

Take Action

Take the T Out of CAN'T

Have Patience

Do What is Right

Your Past is not Equal to Your Future

This Too Shall Pass

Laugh it off

Do What You Love, Love What You Do

Be a Positive Thinker

Have Faith in Yourself

LESSON 18.

Take the T Out of CAN'T

"Replace your I CAN'T attitude with I CAN."

I can't do this, I can't do that. The word *can't* is probably one of those useless words that has stopped many from achieving their true potential. *Can't* shows lack of faith in you.

Everything is possible to those who believe believe it is, to those who have faith. Napoleon Hill said years ago, "Whether you believe you can or you can't, you are right." All you have to do is take the T out of CAN'T. Convert your Cant's into Cans. It all starts with a CAN attitude, an "it's possible" attitude.

As soon as you accept a defeat in your mind, the defeat is pretty much guaranteed. Be mindful of your T's!

I CAN'T win this race.
I CAN'T write.
I CAN'T become a millionaire.
I CAN'T control my thoughts.
I CAN'T THIS, I CAN'T THAT.

CAN'T takes away possibilities. CAN creates them. And all you have to do is remove the T, it is that simple!

147

I CAN win this race.
I CAN write.
I CAN become a millionaire.
I CAN control my thoughts.
I CAN THIS, I CAN THAT

From here on, if anyone tells you that you can't, don't accept it. Listen to them, delete the T, and hear them saying you CAN. Just tune yourself out and don't listen to the T. If they say, "You can't be a millionaire, you hear, "You can be a millionaire." Now buy into what they said (they said, "You can be a millionaire"). Believe in the CAN. Thank them for what they said. Borrow the T from CAN'T, and use it for Thanks. They'll be surprised that you are thanking them for their impossibilities.

"Successful people look for possibilities, failures talk of impossible"
Everything is possible for you. Yes, you can. You can, you can, you can!

Daily Affirmations:

1.

2.

3.

Action Plans:

1.

2.

3.

Start With Gratitude

Take Care of Your Health

Your Attitude Determines Your Destiny

Have Written Goals

Make Every Moment Count

Improve Your Skills Constantly

Know Your Purpose

Give Up a Bad Habit

Take Action

Dream Big! Think Abundant!

Have Patience

Do What is Right

Your Past is not Equal to Your Future

This Too Shall Pass

Laugh it off

Do What You Love, Love What You Do

Be a Positive Thinker

Have Faith in Yourself

Take the T Out of CAN'T

LESSON 19.

Dream Big! Think Abundant!

**"Dreams do come true. Be careful of your dreams.
Make sure they are big"**

This is my favorite topic! Have you ever wished for something and then rejected it as an impossible dream? Have those dreams come true often? And if they do come true, then doesn't it make sense that we dream big?

Our dreams become realities in our subconscious. The subconscious doesn't know real from fake. It hears your dream and stores it in there for the future. Sometimes those dreams manifest in minutes, sometimes they take years. But they do become real more often than not. Your dreams come in the form of wishes and desires. And the right ones keep growing, especially when they are nurtured properly. Our dreams are generated by us and, sadly, suppressed by us, too. "I want a brand new boat," the dream says. "Nope, you can't have it, you don't know boating," our mind says. And the dream dies. But if you don't accept your mind's suggestion and instead, still dream of that boat, that boat will be yours one day.

Be very vivid with your dreams. Make them larger than life. Let them grow and expand. And then let the universe work for you to make it happen for you.

It's been 23 years, and I still vividly remember a dream I had when I landed in the USA. I had a temporary starter job that paid minimum wage. We lived in an apartment. My uncle drove a Mercedes, and I told him that I wanted to get one. His instant response to me was, "First learn how to pronounce the word Mercedes." It's pronounced differently in the US than it is in India, and I learnt that very quickly that day. But I never let that dream die. And 17 years later (although it was possible much sooner), I had my brand new Mercedes. Many such dreams have come true for me, and I am sure it is no different for you either. It's possible for all of us to dream, and to dream BIG. And we should let no one rain on our parade. My uncle's words became an inspiration for me. I had cancelled the T from his indirect can't.

Just like our thoughts, our dreams are our seeds too. Don't let them go to waste. Sow them properly. Big dreams will many times take a little longer to come true, so be patient. Trust that the universe is abundant and that God is personally working towards fulfilling your dream for you.

There is plenty in the universe for all of us. It is possible for all of us to achieve and get what we want. But we must dream big, we must believe in abundance philosophy, and we must have faith in ourselves and faith in God. If we have a big dream of something but then tell ourselves that it is not possible for us, then we have instantly killed that dream. We have not trusted in God's abundance. Believe it is possible for you, and know it is meant for you.

I had a dream of writing a book, and now that it has come

true, I have a dream to write many more. It has not occurred to me that there are too many books out there and that mine may not get published. Why wouldn't it be? It is a life-changing book. It has so many good lessons, lessons that will change the life of many readers. Lessons that have already changed your life or they soon will. And I have dedicated all the profits to a good cause, making my dream even bigger. I will see the results of my profits helping many others. My spirituality will grow and my love for Krishna will expand. And if I can, so can you. I wasn't born into riches, but I was fortunate to be blessed with good values and a great belief system by my parents and grandparents. Regardless of our circumstances, we can all dream big, and we should dream big. Nothing says that you must stay a victim of your current circumstances for the rest of your life. We should have an absolute non-wavering belief that anything is possible for us.

Kill your doubts if there are any, and then see the miracles take place. Know that they will happen, so be patient. Don't do anything wrong to see them happen faster, they will come true in their due course. Don't work against the law of nature. Don't cheat anyone to fulfill your dreams. Do what is right, always. Know that all material things will be left back here when we are gone. Why pay a penalty in our next life for our misdeeds in this life? Dream big, believe in your dreams, do only right and moral things to achieve them, and then see them come true for you.

"Big dreams pay big dividends. Dream big, believe in your dreams."

Dream big and may all your dreams come true. May God bless you with abundant thoughts.

Daily Affirmations:

1.

2.

3.

Action Plans:

1.

2.

3.

Start With Gratitude

Take Care of Your Health

Your Attitude Determines Your Destiny

Have Written Goals

Make Every Moment Count

Improve Your Skills Constantly

Know Your Purpose

Give Up a Bad Habit

Take Action

Have Patience

Build Wealth! Money is Not the Root of Evil

Do What is Right

Your Past is not Equal to Your Future

This Too Shall Pass

Laugh it off

Do What You Love, Love What You Do

Be a Positive Thinker

Have Faith in Yourself

Take the T Out of CAN'T

Dream Big! Think Abundant

LESSON 20.

Build Wealth! Money is Not the Root of Evil

"You can choose to be rich and you can choose to be poor, it is your choice."

There are many books written on monetary wealth creation, so we only want to touch on the basics of money. The first thing we need to do though is to develop and grow ourselves and know the importance and limitations of money. What good is money if the person who has it isn't wise enough to use it properly? But now that you have come to the end of this book, assuming you have read all previous chapters, we know that you are ready to handle a lot of money.

We have all heard at one time or another, that money is the root of all evil. That is far from the truth. The *abuse* of money, the *misuse of power* gained due to money, the *greed* caused by money, the desire to make money *at any cost and at anyone's expense*—these are the roots of evil. Money, when made for the right reasons, and to help humanity and mankind, is a very good thing. It is really the *lack* of money that creates more problems, not the abundance of money. Look at most riots, thefts, and murders, and you will see lack of money, or importance to money for the wrong reasons, is always the cause of the unrest.

So here are some lessons about building wealth. They are one-liners, so read relevant books for details.

About Money:
1. Money is not the root of all evil, misuse of money is.
2. Money is important and necessary for all good causes.
3. We can not help others without money.
4. It is okay to make money honestly.
5. Never be ashamed of making too much money, but don't hoard it. Use it to help others. Make it and give it away.
6. Don't be caught up in greed or false pride. What is yours today is not yours tomorrow.
7. Don't be attached to money or material things.

About Building Wealth:

1. Work hard. There is no substitute for it.
2. Make your money work hard for you. Use the principles of compound interest in your favor.
3. Invest wisely. Don't make get-rich-quick investments based on greed.
4. Invest in real estate, especially your primary home.
5. Pay off higher interest loans with lower rate offerings. Get out of debt if possible.
6. Tax deductibility is not a reason to buy anything. Buy something only if you need it. Paying $100 in interest to get a $25 tax break makes no sense. You still lost $75.
7. Protect your assets with necessary insurance, but don't over insure.
8. Make saving a habit. Put 10-15% of your income, and more if possible, towards savings. You will never

miss the money if you do it right from the top, and you will never do it if you wait to save from what is left over.

9. Back to compound interest again. This is huge. Understand it well. Compound interest, in time, does miracles. Let's show you how.

Let's say you save $200/month for the next 30 years at 0% interest. At the end of 30 years you will have $72,000. If you changed that to 50 years, you will have $120,000. Not bad with little discipline.

But now let's see this differently. Save $200/month for 30 years at 7% interest, you will have $245,000 at the end of 30 years. Compare this to $72,000 at 0% interest. At $200/month saved for 50 years at 7% interest, you will have $1,096,000. Compare that to a mere $120,000 at 0%.

But let's change this a little. $200/month for 30 years at 12% gives $706,000. $200/month for 50 years at 12% gives $7,890,000—WOW! Amount, time, and interest make all the difference.

Let's change the amount to $500/month. $500/month for 30 years at 7% is $614,000. The same at 12% is $1,765,000. $500/month for 50 years at 7% is $2,740,000. The same at 12% is 19,725,000—WOW!

Start saving early. Look for the highest interest rate possible (in a relatively safe investment). And keep it growing as long as you can.

10. Don't waste things, whether they cost you or whether they are free. When at a hotel, turn off the room lights when leaving. When eating at an all-you-can-eat buffet, only take what you can eat, go for a refill if you want to, but don't take too much only to throw

it way. Disciplines become habits. Small acts become habits. When you do for others, you will do it for yourself too.

11.   Passive income is better than active income. Passive is when your money or your past efforts produce money. Active is when you have to be working to make money. A job is active, investment property is passive. Patented product is passive.

12.   Set a budget. Know how and where to spend your money. Spend it where necessary regardless of the cost. Don't waste it where it is not necessary, regardless of how cheap it is.

13.   Save towards your retirement. Take advantage of tax sheltered growth. See your savings multiply many folds years later.

14.   Teach your children and loved ones the value of money. That's the best gift you can give them

"Become wealthy in style. Give it all away in style too."

Plan to give it all away to causes that are dear to your heart. And please don't give them a fish. Show them how to fish.

Daily Affirmations:

1.

2.

3.

Action Plans:

1.

2.

3.

Start With Gratitude

Take Care of Your Health

Your Attitude Determines Your Destiny

Have Written Goals

Make Every Moment Count

Improve Your Skills Constantly

Know Your Purpose

Give Up a Bad Habit

Take Action

Have Patience

Give More Than you Promise

Do What is Right

Your Past is not Equal to Your Future

This Too Shall Pass

Laugh it off

Do What You Love, Love What You Do

Be a Positive Thinker

Have Faith in Yourself

Take the T Out of CAN'T

Dream Big! Think Abundant!

Build Wealth! Money is Not the Root of Evil

LESSON 21.

Give More Than you Promise

"Over promise and then over deliverer."

After lesson 10, we told you that lessons 11-20 were bonus lessons. That was good; but not good enough for me. Therefore I have added this lesson, appropriately titled, 'Give More Than You Promise'.

When we give what we promise, we are ordinary. When we give a little *extra*, we become *extra*ordinary. The little extra makes all the difference. Make it your life goal to always do more than what is expected of you, and never ever less.

Give a little more at your job.
Pay a little more attention to your studies.
Take a little extra care of your wealth and your health.
Do a little extra in your community.
Give a little extra for charity.
Pray a little extra to God everyday.

A little extra daily compounds to a lot in time. Think of the gold medalists. A little extra effort by the one who gets gold vs. the one who gets silver (many times that extra is only a tenth of a second lead) is worth millions of dollars. And that very little lead time was the result of the little extra everyday for many years. While giving a little extra makes a huge difference to our present and future potential, giving a little less than required robs us of our self esteem and our confidence. And if all it takes is a little extra, then why not? Make it a firm commitment from here on to give all you have and then a little more. And then a little more, please.

Before we conclude, here are a few more extras:

1. Don't be realistic. Only unrealistic people exceed their dreams.
2. WOW them. Let your work, whatever it is, generate a WOW for you. Give your very best to earn a WOW.
3. Always be a student. Keep learning. Never stop growing. We are either growing or dying.
4. Pull people up, not down. You have to be in a higher position to be able to pull them up. To pull them down, you to have to first get down. Why would you want to get down just to bring them down?
5. Make your life's balance sheet. Know your real blessings (your assets) and the perceived hurts (your liabilities). Why do we call the hurts "perceived hurts"? Because nothing has a meaning except the meaning we give to it. A sound mind, a healthy heart, these are all blessings.
6. Be different. Don't conform to others just to blend in especially when you know it is not right. Create your own path that leads many in the right direction.
7. Serve the needy. Always be looking for ways to give back. A humble way of giving back is to not even call it giving. Call it retuning. God gave to us, we can only return. Who are we to give?
8. Live an exemplary life. Be a role model.

9.   Have a mentor. Be a mentor.
10. Don't worry, be happy. Life is short, enjoy it.
11. Always be thankful for your blessings. Always!
12. Begin your day by thanking God for His blessings. End your day with thanks too.

"Start your day remembering God. End your day with thanks to Him."

May God bless you with joy and courage. May you spread the same around the world. Go out and make a difference. YOU CAN!

ACKNOWLEDGEMENT

There are many authors I have read and many speakers I have listened to and I thank them all for who I am today. But there are few I must personally thank through this book. I thank Jim Rohn my mentor. And I thank Howard Brinton, Les Brown, Stephen Covey, Deepak Chopra, Wayne Dyer, T. Harv Eker, Jeffery Gitomer, Tom Hopkins, Harvey Mckay, Zig Ziglar and many others. You have made a difference in my life and I am sure have touched lives of many others.

My thanks also to my parents for the value system they have instilled in me. And my thanks to my wife, my sisters, and my kids for their help and support in everything I have attempted.

My thanks also to Victor and Jessica for helping me on this book writing project.

My thanks to all those who reviewed this book before it got published. And my thanks to everyone at Book Surge, especially John , Julie and Thomas for all their assistance.

Last, but not the least, my thanks to Lord Krishna for all His blessings. He is too good. This couldn't have been possible without HIS inspiration.

ABOUT THE AUTHOR

Born in New Delhi, India, Sanjeev migrated to USA in 1982, at the age of 23. Before coming to the USA, he had completed his Electrical Engineering from YMCA Institute of Engineering, and worked briefly for Siemens in New Delhi.

When in USA, Sanjeev took on different starter jobs for first few months till he landed a position at Unilux, Inc in Hackensack, NJ. That is where his career developed under the strong leadership of President Bill Blethen. Sanjeev traveled the world, many times over, training others and setting up satellite offices. After growing the department many folds, he decided to pursue a different career and went into real estate in 1992 and then never looked back. His hard work and commitment to serve clients with a WOW made him an overnight success. He received many awards and recognitions for his work. He served at many levels in local, state and national levels and was named 'Realtor of the Year' by New Jersey Association of Realtors in 2004.

Sanjeev has read many books and attended many seminars. He says, "If we are not growing, we are dying" and he pursues becoming the very best at all times. A true positive thinker, he never sees a glass half empty. He has experienced continued personal, professional and financial success through his winning combination of attitude and generosity. And now his dream is to help others grow and meet the needs of those who need the resources, specially the poor kids. He says "I have been blessed with a lot, by Krishna's mercy, and now it is time to give back (he actually calls it return back, as returning keeps it humble).

Sanjeev lives in New Jersey with his parents, wife, and two kids, a daughter and a son. You can reach him by e-mailing him at sanjeev@sanjeevaneja.com.

THE READER'S SAY

"One should not embark on a journey for self without this very valuable guidebook to help lead the way"

Glenn C. Slavin, Esq....trial lawyer, life coach and father of two

"WOW, what a workbook. This should be a must read manual for everyone. Simple yet very important lessons, so well put in one place"

Dr Satyapal Gandotra, MD, Diabetes Specialist, Krishna devotee

"As a physician, I have always tried to heal the body and soul with God's guidance. In this book, Sanjeev has outlined the pathway very succinctly. A real commendable job"

Dr S. Prasad, MD, Chairman, Department of Medicine